U.S.A. TRAVEL GUIDES

VERMONT

BY ANN HEINRICHS • ILLUSTRATED BY MATT KANIA

The Child's World®
childsworld.com

Published by The Child's World®
1980 Lookout Drive • Mankato, MN 56003-1705
800-599-READ • www.childsworld.com

Photo Credits
Photographs ©: Don Land/Shutterstock Images, cover;
Jay Boucher/Shutterstock Images, 7; Kevin M. Walsh/
iStockphoto, 8; Ken Sturm/USFWS, 11; Deborah Ann
Joaquim, 12; Matt Howry CC2.0, 15; Andre Jenny Stock
Connection Worldwide/Newscom, 16, 23; David Wilson
CC2.0, 19; liz west CC2.0, 20; Shutterstock Images, 24,
27, 37 (top), 37 (bottom); Abigail Batchelder CC2.0,
28; daveynin CC2.0, 31; Edward Fielding/Shutterstock
Images, 32; Alexander Sviridov/Shutterstock Images, 35

ISBN 9781503819856
LCCN 2016961197

Printing
Printed in the United States of America
PA02334

Ann Heinrichs is the author of more than 100 books for children and young adults. She has also enjoyed successful careers as a children's book editor and an advertising copywriter. Ann grew up in Fort Smith, Arkansas, and lives in Chicago, Illinois.

post card

About the Author
Ann Heinrichs

Matt Kania loves maps and, as a kid, dreamed of making them. In school he studied geography and cartography, and today he makes maps for a living. Matt's favorite thing about drawing maps is learning about the places they represent. Many of the maps he has created can be found in books, magazines, videos, Web sites, and public places.

post card

About the
Map Illustrator
Matt Kania

On the cover: Stowe, Vermont is a popular place to visit in fall.

OUR VERMONT TRIP

Get ready to explore the Green Mountain State. That's Vermont! You'll find lots to see and do there.

You'll watch people making maple syrup. You'll climb mountains and wander through forests. You'll watch woodworkers and stonecutters. You'll see how ice cream is made. And you'll build your very own teddy bear!

Does that sound like your kind of fun? Then let's get going. Just follow that loopy dotted line. Or else skip around. Either way, you're in for a great adventure. Now, buckle up and hang on tight. We're off to see Vermont!

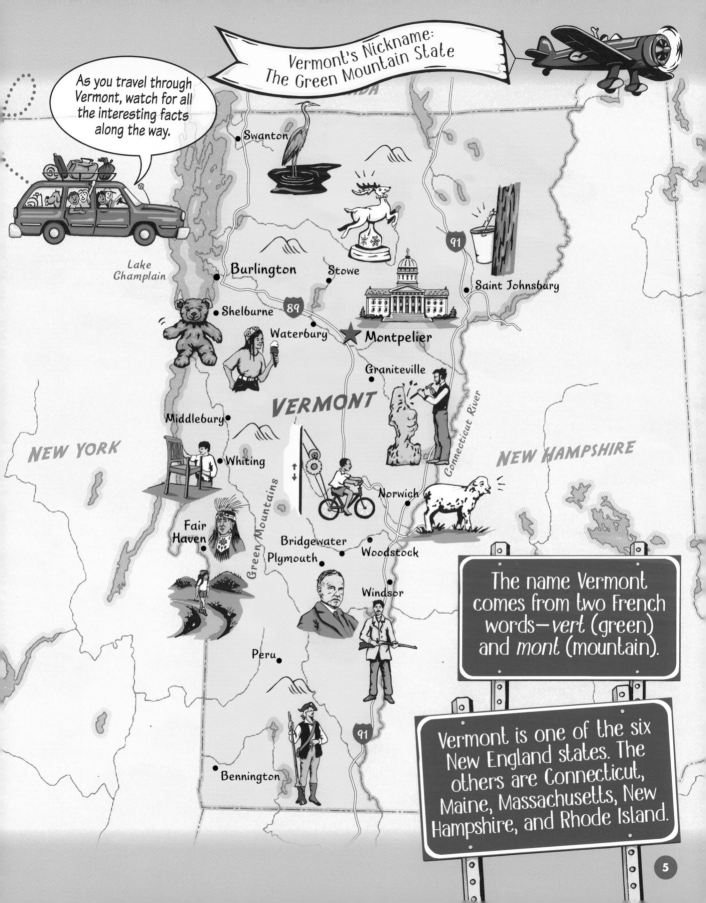

CANADA

Parts of Lake Champlain belong to Vermont, New York, and Canada.

Isle La Motte

Grand Isle

Franklin County

Mount Mansfield

Lake Champlain

NEW YORK

Green Mountains

Appalachian Trail

Highest Temperature: Vernon July 7, 1912 107°F (42°C)

Bloomfield

Lowest Temperature: Bloomfield December 30, 1933 -50°F (-46°C)

Connecticut River

NEW HAMPSHIRE

Let's stop at Hapgood Pond! It's a recreation area. We can swim, fish, and camp out there.

The Appalachian Trail runs through Vermont. This hiking path extends all the way from Maine to Georgia.

• Mount Tabor
• Peru

Hapgood Pond

Vernon

MASSACHUSETTS

HIGHEST AND LOWEST POINTS
HIGHEST: Mount Mansfield at 4,393 feet (1,339 m)
LOWEST: Lake Champlain in Franklin County at 95 feet (29 m)

Grand Isle and Isle La Motte are islands in Lake Champlain. They belong to Vermont.

EXPLORING THE GREEN MOUNTAINS

Take a drive in the Green Mountains. They're so big, you could start anywhere. Traveling between Peru and Mount Tabor is fun. You'll wind through dense forests. Deer and foxes might peek out at you!

The Green Mountains are like Vermont's backbone. They run down the center of the state. Northeastern Vermont is rugged and hilly. Many mountains here are made of granite. That's a valuable building stone.

The Connecticut River forms Vermont's eastern border. Land in the river valley is very fertile. Lake Champlain creates part of the western border. Land along the lake makes great farmland, too.

Do you like to hike? The Green Mountains are a popular hiking destination.

STOWE'S WINTER CARNIVAL

Ice carvers hack and saw away. They're making spectacular ice sculptures. Want to play snow volleyball? Or join the snowshoe race? You can find all of these events at the Stowe Winter Carnival!

Many Vermont towns hold winter carnivals. They celebrate all kinds of winter sports. Vermont's a great place for skiing. It's also great for sleigh rides through the snow.

When it's warmer, people go biking, hiking, or boating. Thousands of tourists visit Vermont in the fall. They come to see the changing leaves. The orange, red, and yellow leaves are awesome!

You'll find plenty of winter activities to do in Stowe.

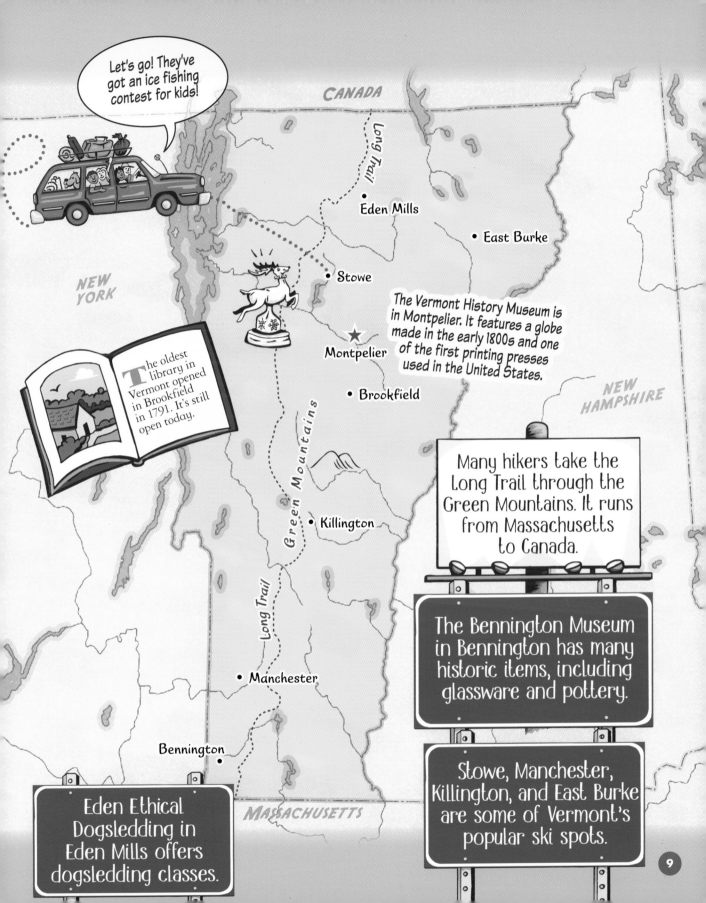

Missisquoi National Wildlife Refuge
• Swanton

CANADA

Is that a woodcock or a grouse? Both are plump and feed on the ground. Is its bill really long? Then it's a woodcock. Is its bill really short? Then it's a grouse.

Green Mountains

Black terns nest at Missisquoi National Wildlife Refuge. They're a type of sea bird.

NEW YORK

NEW HAMPSHIRE

The National Park Service has two sites in Vermont.

Male woodcocks do a dance to attract females. They circle into the air and then dive toward the ground. Their feathers make a whistling sound as they dive.

Snowshoe hares have mostly brown fur in the summer. They're almost all white in the winter. Then they blend in with their snowy surroundings.

Missisquoi is an Abenaki Native American word meaning "great grassy meadow."

Do you like watching birds? Check out Missisquoi National Wildlife Refuge near Swanton. You'll see countless birds there!

More than 20,000 ducks pass through in the fall. Hundreds of long-legged blue herons nest there, too. They build nests out of sticks in trees. Many songbirds twitter across the meadows. And graceful hawks soar overhead.

Want to see lots of wild animals? Just wander through the Green Mountains. Deer, foxes, and coyotes make their homes there. Even moose, bobcats, and bears roam around. Snowshoe hares go bounding through the winter snow. They have great big feet!

This peregrine falcon calls Missisquoi National Wildlife Refuge home.

You hear drums beat and flute music. Native Americans march in with flags. War **veterans** carry American flags. Others carry flags that show their tribe or nation. You're watching the grand entry parade at the Wildfire Phillips Return to Spirit Intertribal Powwow in Fair Haven.

Abenakis from Vermont and Native Americans from all over the country attend this powwow. An Abenaki descendant named Deborah "Wildfire Phillips" Joaquim and her family host it every year. The powwow celebrates Native American identities and traditions.

Native Americans have lived in Vermont for thousands of years. There are approximately 2,500 Native Americans living in Vermont today.

People with Native American heritage attend the Wildfire Phillips Powwow.

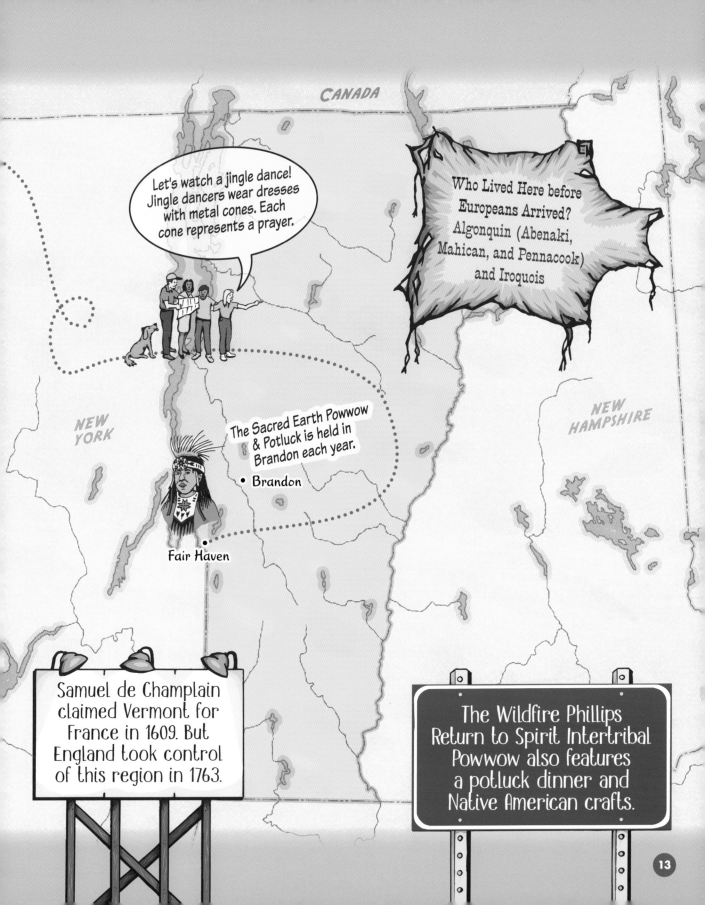

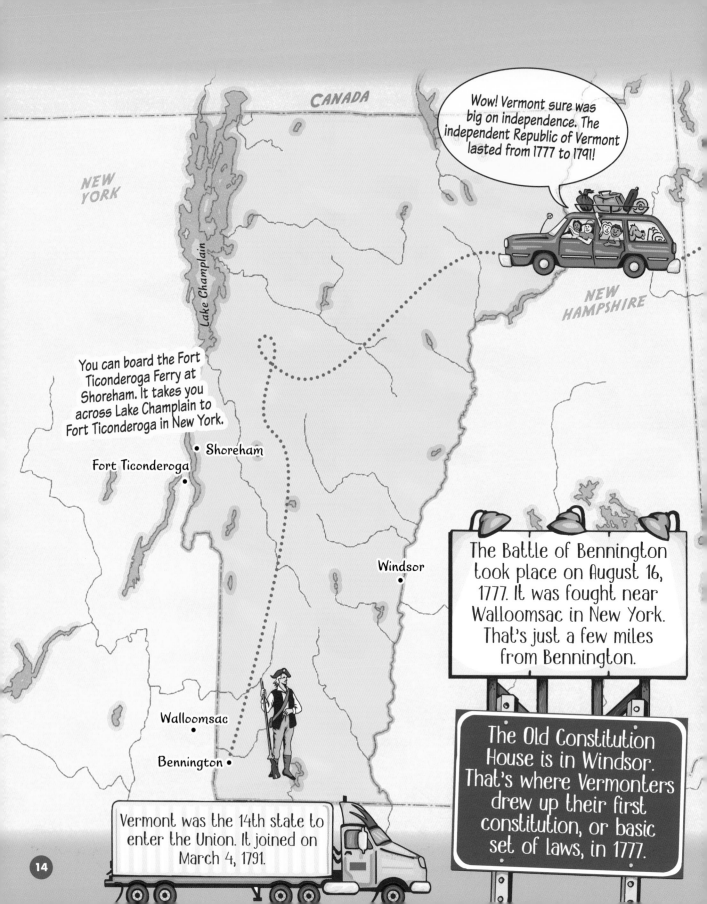

THE BATTLE OF BENNINGTON AND THE REVOLUTIONARY WAR

C limb to the top of the Bennington Battle Monument. You can see for miles! This monument honors a famous battle. It took place during the Revolutionary War (1775–1783). **Colonists** fought this war for freedom from England.

Vermonter Ethan Allen organized the Green Mountain Boys. They fought bravely in many battles. One was at Fort Ticonderoga in New York. Another was the Battle of Bennington. The British lost this battle—and the war.

Vermont had never been a separate colony. It declared its own independence in 1777. Vermont remained an independent **republic** for 14 years.

Want to learn about soldiers who fought for freedom? Visit the Bennington Battle Monument.

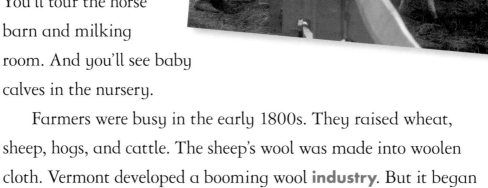

What was early farm life like in Vermont? Just visit Billings Farm and Museum in Woodstock. You'll see woolly sheep and mooing cows. You'll tour the horse barn and milking room. And you'll see baby calves in the nursery.

Farmers were busy in the early 1800s. They raised wheat, sheep, hogs, and cattle. The sheep's wool was made into woolen cloth. Vermont developed a booming wool **industry**. But it began declining in the 1870s.

Then dairy farming expanded. Many dairy farms spread out across the Champlain Valley. Milk, butter, and cheese became important Vermont products.

Learn about Vermont's farming industry when you visit Billings Farm and Museum.

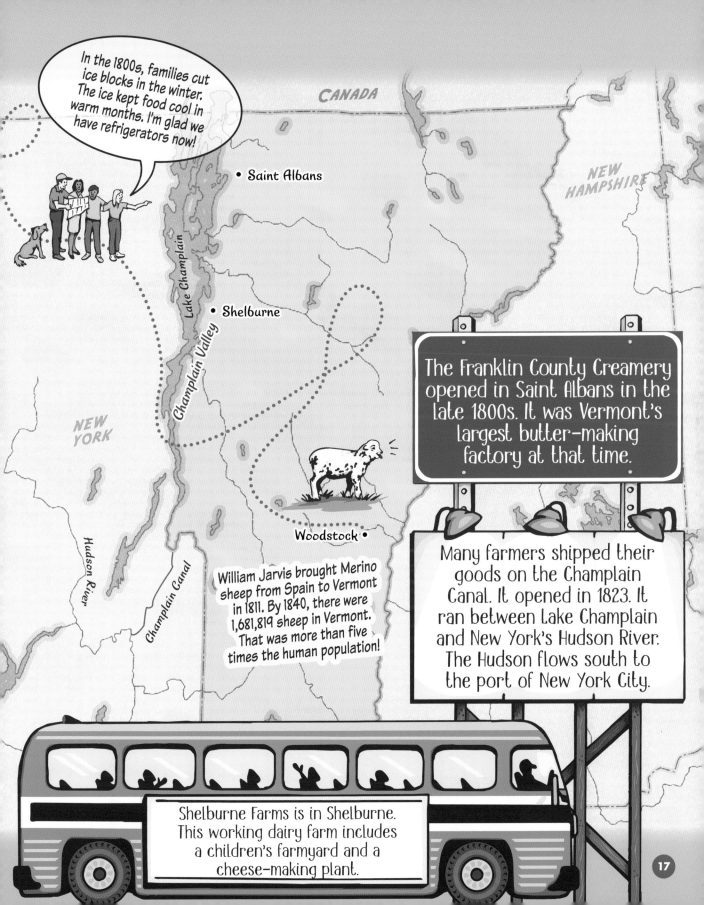

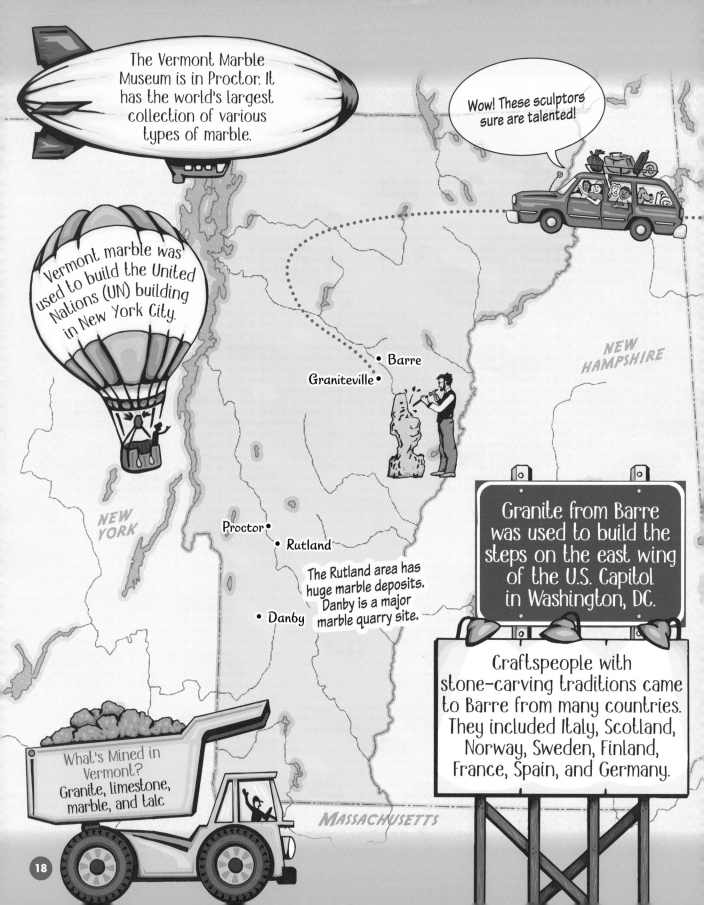

The Vermont Marble Museum is in Proctor. It has the world's largest collection of various types of marble.

Wow! These sculptors sure are talented!

Vermont marble was used to build the United Nations (UN) building in New York City.

NEW HAMPSHIRE

• Barre
Graniteville •

NEW YORK

Proctor •
• Rutland

The Rutland area has huge marble deposits. Danby is a major marble quarry site.

• Danby

Granite from Barre was used to build the steps on the east wing of the U.S. Capitol in Washington, DC.

Craftspeople with stone-carving traditions came to Barre from many countries. They included Italy, Scotland, Norway, Sweden, Finland, France, Spain, and Germany.

What's Mined in Vermont? Granite, limestone, marble, and talc

MASSACHUSETTS

THE ROCK OF AGES QUARRY

Gaze down into the pit. A 60-story building would fit in this hole! Workers are cutting out massive blocks of stone.

This is the Rock of Ages **quarry**. It's in Graniteville. Be sure to visit the quarry's design studio. You'll see master sculptors carving the granite. They make statues, monuments, and grave markers.

The city of Barre's first granite quarry opened in about 1815. By the late 1800s, many quarries had opened throughout Vermont. Expert stone carvers began arriving from Italy. In their hands, the granite took shape. They created beautiful statues and artistic designs. Some of their descendants still work in Barre today.

What is granite used for? Find out at the Rock of Ages Quarry.

WINDSOR'S AMERICAN PRECISION MUSEUM

Vermont became an early leader in manufacturing. Its textile mills spun raw wool into woolen goods. Then Vermonters developed a new kind of factory. You'll learn about it at the American **Precision** Museum in Windsor. It's in the old Robbins and Lawrence **Armory**.

People once made rifles by hand. But Robbins and Lawrence made them by machine. They made each part in a standard size. Then rifles could be built and repaired easily. This began the machine tool industry.

Machine tools are factory machines. They cut, grind, or bore holes. Today, they're used in making many factory goods.

Visit the American Precision Museum. You'll see what factories were like in the 1800s.

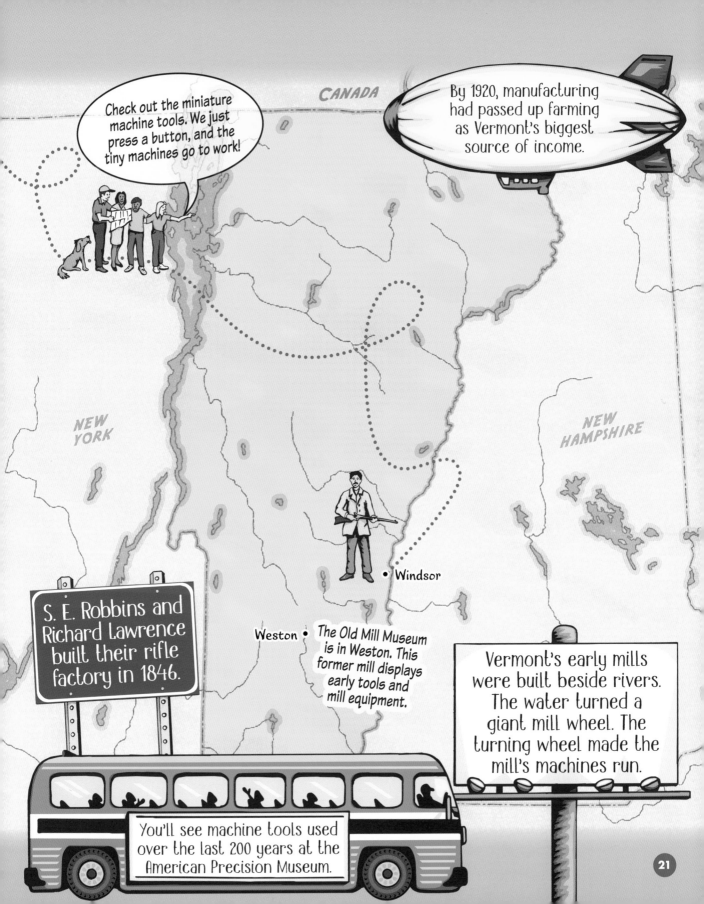

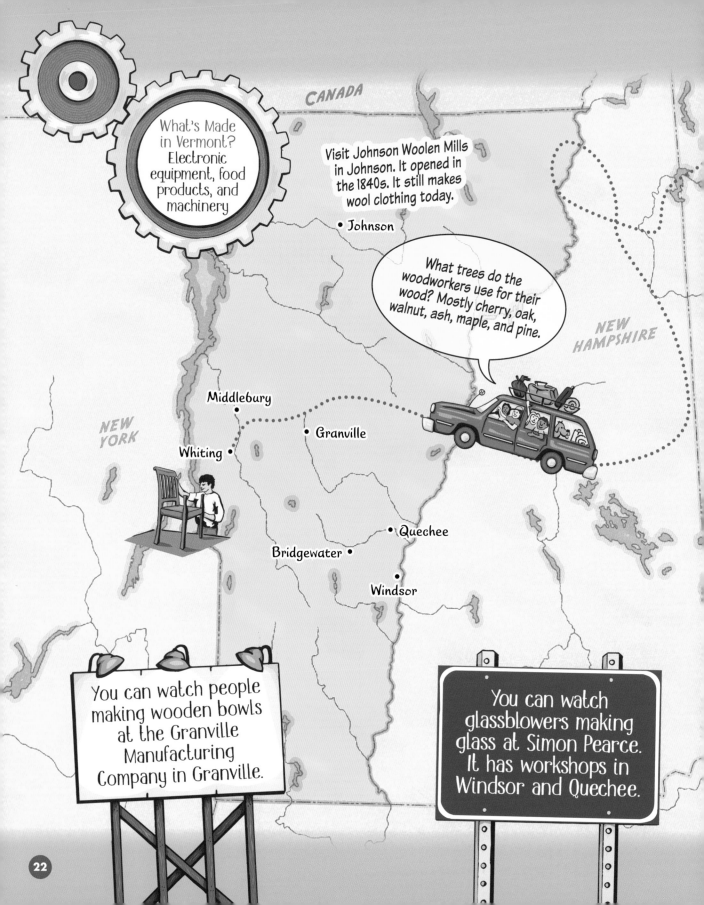

CANADA

What's Made in Vermont? Electronic equipment, food products, and machinery

Visit Johnson Woolen Mills in Johnson. It opened in the 1840s. It still makes wool clothing today.

• Johnson

What trees do the woodworkers use for their wood? Mostly cherry, oak, walnut, ash, maple, and pine.

NEW HAMPSHIRE

NEW YORK

Middlebury

• Granville

Whiting •

• Quechee

Bridgewater •

Windsor

You can watch people making wooden bowls at the Granville Manufacturing Company in Granville.

You can watch glassblowers making glass at Simon Pearce. It has workshops in Windsor and Quechee.

Where can you watch woodworkers in Vermont? Lots of places! Try Cotswold Furniture Makers in Whiting or the ShackletonThomas furniture workshop in Bridgewater. People are crafting wooden furniture at both places. You'll really like Maple Landmark Woodcraft in Middlebury. It makes wooden toys and games!

Wood products are important Vermont factory goods. Even in the 1800s, Vermont's sawmills were busy. They cut logs into lumber.

Today, electrical equipment is the top factory item. That includes computer parts. Food products are really important, too. That includes cheese and ice cream!

Sawmills in Vermont cut logs for use in furniture and other wood products.

Step into the state capitol in Montpelier. You'll see paintings of two U.S. presidents. They're Chester A. Arthur and Calvin Coolidge. Why are they here? Because both were born in Vermont!

The capitol is the center of Vermont's state government. Vermont has three branches of government. One branch makes the state's laws. Its members belong to the General Assembly. The governor heads another branch of government. This branch's job is to carry out the laws. Judges make up the third branch. They know the laws well. They decide whether someone has broken a law.

The capitol's golden dome sparkles in the sun.

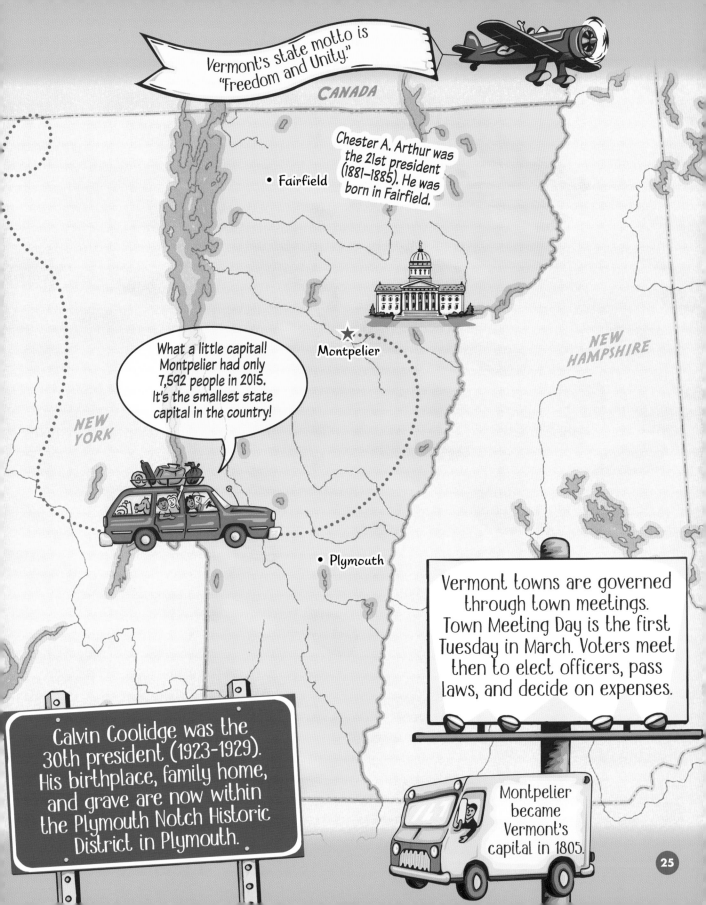

CANADA

Let's check out the Coolidge Homestead. That's where Coolidge was sworn in as president at 2:47 A.M. He must have been really sleepy!

In 2016, 624,594 people lived in Vermont. It's the 49th-largest state by population.

Burlington • • Essex

South Burlington

NEW YORK

NEW HAMPSHIRE

• Plymouth

Plymouth Notch is a little village within the town of Plymouth.

Population of Largest Cities
Burlington.................42,452
Essex.........................20,946
South Burlington..........18,791

Calvin Coolidge was the only president born on the 4th of July! Plymouth holds a 4th of July parade in his honor.

Warren Harding, the 29th president, died on August 2, 1923. Coolidge, his vice president, was sworn in as president in the early hours of August 3.

Vermont welcomed many **immigrants** in the late 1800s. They came from Italy, Scotland, Finland, Canada, and many other countries. They found jobs in factories and in the lumber, marble, and granite industries.

MASSACHUSETTS

SILENT CAL AND PLYMOUTH NOTCH

Stroll around Plymouth Notch. President Calvin Coolidge was born here. He wandered the same streets as a boy. He even took the oath to become president here! Coolidge was a man of few words. He was known as Silent Cal.

People saw Coolidge as a typical Yankee. That's a term often used for New Englanders. Early Yankee settlers built homes in the wilderness. They invented clever ways to solve problems. They were careful with money.

Most Vermonters still live in **rural** areas. Vermont has a small population, too. Only Wyoming has fewer people.

Calvin Coolidge was born in this house in Plymouth Notch.

Make pennies spin around like planets. Pedal a bike to raise an elevator. Take a trip through the human body. You can explore lots more hands-on science activities. Just visit the Montshire Museum of Science in Norwich!

Science discoveries brought Vermont into modern times. International Business Machines (IBM) opened a factory there. It began making computer chips in 1964. By 1971, IBM was Vermont's largest employer.

Many new businesses opened in the state. Today, Vermont's largest employer is the University of Vermont Medical Center in Burlington.

Want to be a scientist someday? Explore fun exhibits at the Montshire Museum of Science.

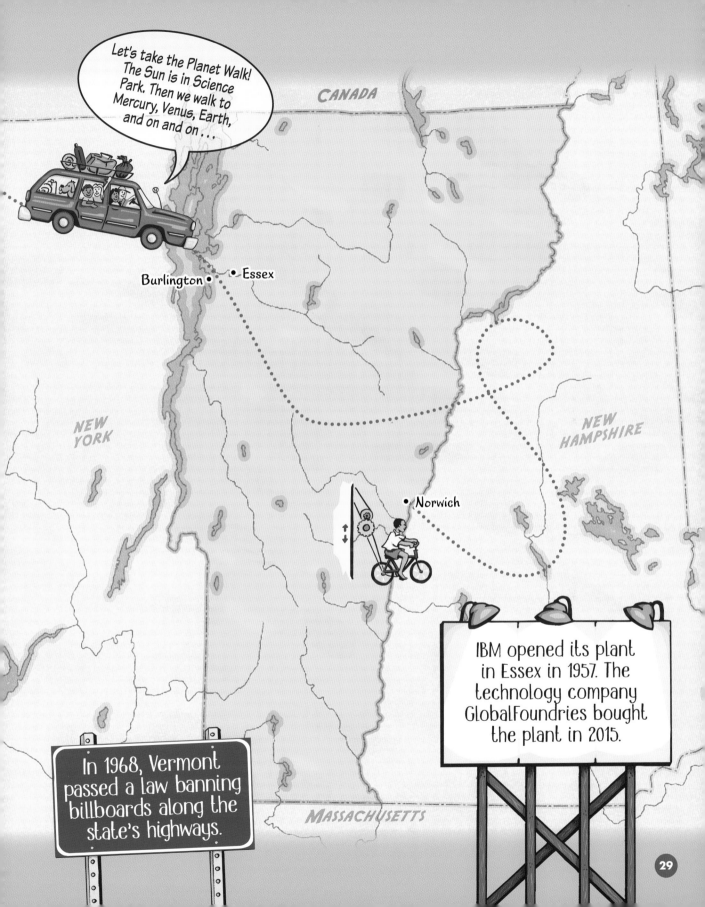

Let's visit the Flavor Graveyard! It's full of little fake tombstones. Each one has the name of a flavor that's no longer made!

CANADA

Enosburg Falls

NEW HAMPSHIRE

In 2015, there were about 260,000 cows in Vermont.

Waterbury • ★ Montpelier

NEW YORK

The state fair is held in Rutland in August each year.

Ben and Jerry are Ben Cohen and Jerry Greenfield. They were childhood friends. They opened their ice cream company in 1978.

• Rutland

Mount Holly

• Grafton

You can see how dairy products are made at Cabot Creamery in Montpelier, Grafton Village Cheese in Grafton, and Crowley Cheese in Mount Holly.

What Does Vermont Raise? Dairy cattle, beef cattle, greenhouse and nursery products, corn, apples, potatoes, and maple syrup

The Vermont Dairy Festival is held in Enosburg Falls.

BEN AND JERRY'S ICE CREAM IN WATERBURY

Start off in the Cow Over the Moon Theater. There you'll see a moo-vie! Next, watch the ice cream factory in action. Finally, head for the Flavo-Room. There you'll sample delicious ice cream treats. You're touring Ben and Jerry's Ice Cream in Waterbury!

Dairy farming is Vermont's leading farm activity. Can you guess what the state beverage is? Milk, of course! Some of that milk becomes butter and cheese. And some ends up as ice cream!

Other Vermont farmers raise crops. Potatoes and corn are the top crops. Apples are the state's major fruit.

Looking for a tasty tour? Head to Ben and Jerry's Ice Cream!

THE SUGAR HOUSE MUSEUM AT MAPLE GROVE FARMS

Have you ever wondered how to make maple syrup? Visit the Sugar House Museum in Saint Johnsbury to find out. This museum is part of Maple Grove Farms. Maple Grove Farms makes its own maple syrup.

Farm workers boil maple **sap** in huge tanks. Then they pour the syrup into jugs. The syrup can be made into many kinds of food—including candy! You'll find many maple products at the Maple Grove Farms gift shop. Bring along your sweet tooth!

Vermont is famous for its delicious maple syrup. Syrup-making time is called sugaring season. It lasts from about late February to mid-April. The sap is drawn from maple trees. Then it's boiled into syrup in a sugar house. A sugary smell fills the air!

Vermont's syrup-making season starts in winter.

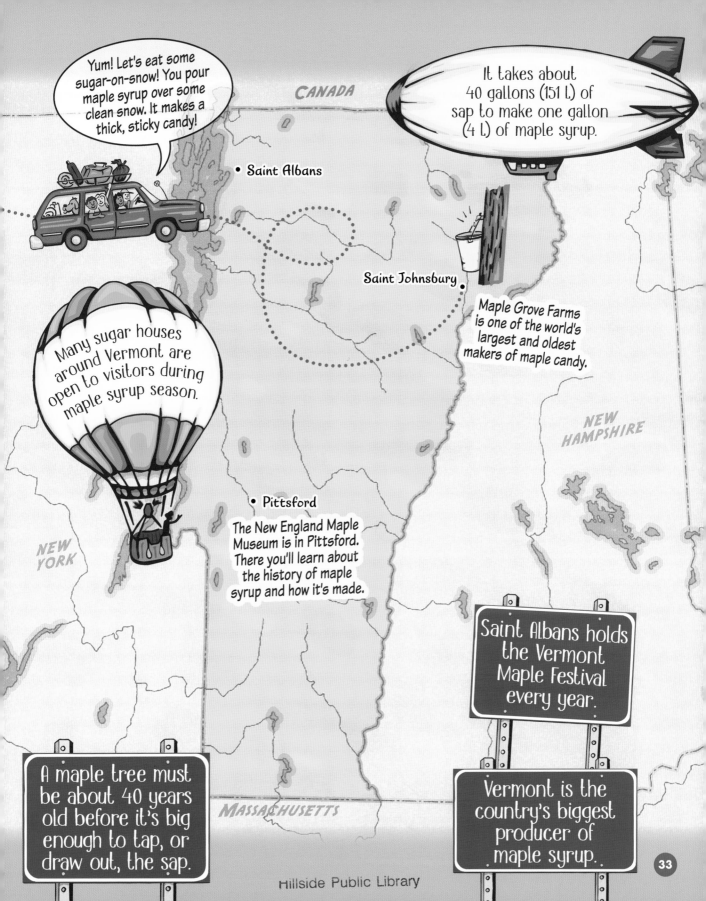

Yum! Let's eat some sugar-on-snow! You pour maple syrup over some clean snow. It makes a thick, sticky candy!

It takes about 40 gallons (151 L) of sap to make one gallon (4 L) of maple syrup.

CANADA

• Saint Albans

Saint Johnsbury •

Maple Grove Farms is one of the world's largest and oldest makers of maple candy.

Many sugar houses around Vermont are open to visitors during maple syrup season.

NEW HAMPSHIRE

• Pittsford

The New England Maple Museum is in Pittsford. There you'll learn about the history of maple syrup and how it's made.

NEW YORK

Saint Albans holds the Vermont Maple Festival every year.

A maple tree must be about 40 years old before it's big enough to tap, or draw out, the sap.

MASSACHUSETTS

Vermont is the country's biggest producer of maple syrup.

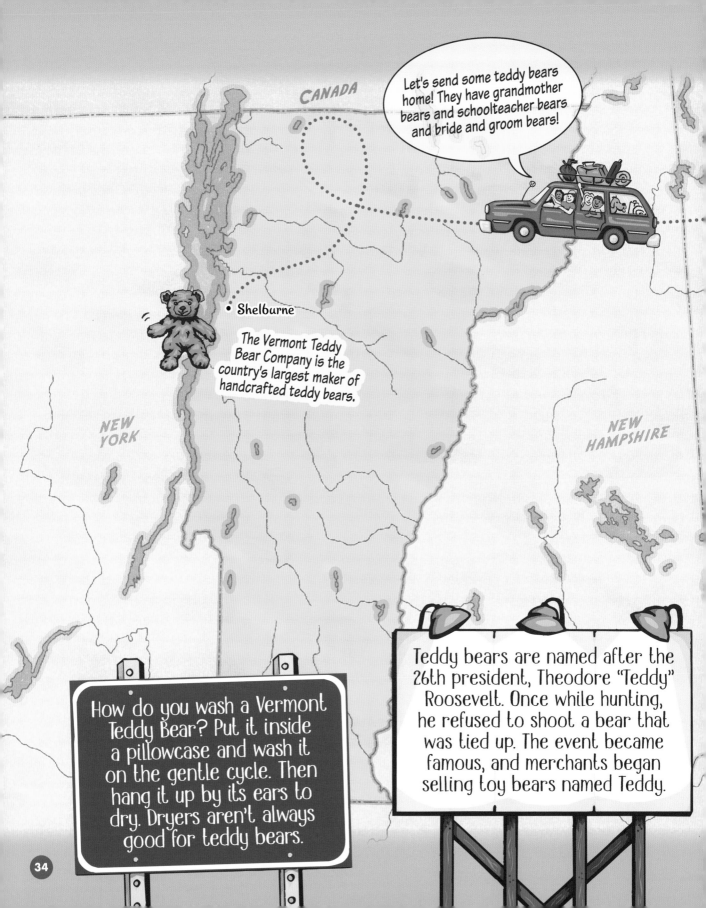

CANADA

Let's send some teddy bears home! They have grandmother bears and schoolteacher bears and bride and groom bears!

• Shelburne

The Vermont Teddy Bear Company is the country's largest maker of handcrafted teddy bears.

NEW YORK

NEW HAMPSHIRE

How do you wash a Vermont Teddy Bear? Put it inside a pillowcase and wash it on the gentle cycle. Then hang it up by its ears to dry. Dryers aren't always good for teddy bears.

Teddy bears are named after the 26th president, Theodore "Teddy" Roosevelt. Once while hunting, he refused to shoot a bear that was tied up. The event became famous, and merchants began selling toy bears named Teddy.

SHELBURNE'S VERMONT TEDDY BEAR FACTORY

Big machines cut the furry fabric. Then people stitch it up on sewing machines. Stuffers fill the forms to make them plump. Then dressers add cute outfits. What are the finished products? Lovable teddy bears!

You're touring the Vermont Teddy Bear factory in Shelburne. It makes hundreds of kinds of bears. They come in all sizes, too.

You can even make your own bear there. Do you like your bears stiff or floppy? You can add stuffing till it's just right. You make a wish. You give your bear a heart. Then it's ready to take home and love!

The Vermont Teddy Bear Company makes about 500,000 teddy bears each year!

When did the oldest library in Vermont open? *See page 9 for the answer.*

What is the difference between a woodcock and a grouse? *Page 10 has the answer.*

When did Vermont become a state? *See page 14 for the answer.*

What's mined in Vermont? *Look on page 18 for the answer.*

When did Montpelier become Vermont's capital? *Page 25 has the answer.*

When was Calvin Coolidge sworn in as president? *Turn to page 26 for the answer.*

What's sugar-on-snow? *Look on page 33 for the answer.*

Who is the country's largest producer of handcrafted teddy bears? *Turn to page 34 for the answer.*

We visited many amazing places on our trip! We also met a lot of interesting people along the way. Look at the map below. Use your finger to trace all the places we have been.

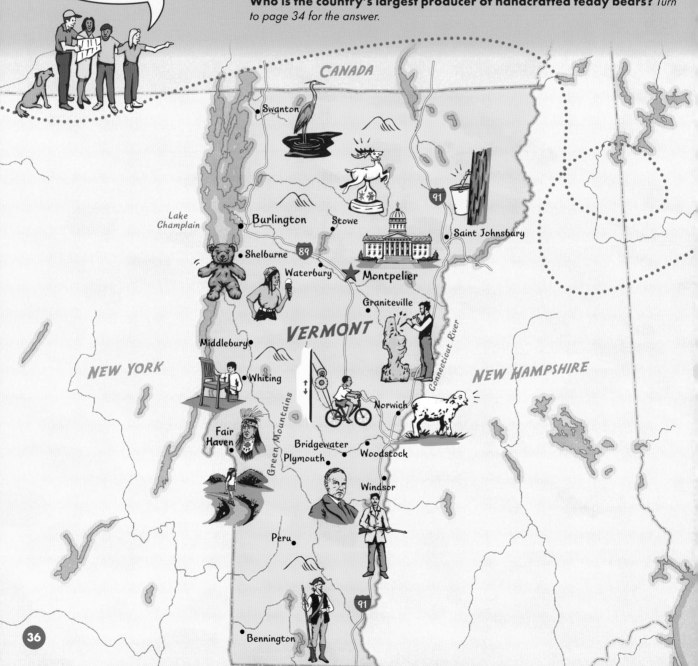

CANADA

Swanton

Lake Champlain

Burlington

Stowe

Saint Johnsbury

91

89

Shelburne

Waterbury

Montpelier

Graniteville

VERMONT

Middlebury

NEW YORK

Whiting

Norwich

NEW HAMPSHIRE

Connecticut River

Green Mountains

Fair Haven

Bridgewater

Plymouth

Woodstock

Windsor

Peru

91

Bennington

State flag

State seal

STATE SYMBOLS

State animal: Morgan horse

State beverage: Milk

State bird: Hermit thrush

State butterfly: Monarch butterfly

State fishes: Brook trout and walleye pike

State flower: Red clover

State fossil: White whale

State fruit: Apple

State gem: Grossular garnet

State insect: Honeybee

State mineral: Talc

State pie: Apple pie

State rocks: Granite, marble, and slate

State soil: Tunbridge soil series

State tree: Sugar maple

That was a great trip! We have traveled all over Vermont! There are a few places that we didn't have time for, though. Next time, we plan to visit the Fairbanks Museum and Planetarium in Saint Johnsbury. Visitors can study the stars or view exhibits related to nature. The museum also contains several artifacts from different world cultures.

STATE SONG

"THESE GREEN MOUNTAINS"
Words and music by Diane Martin

These green hills and silver waters
Are my home—they belong to me
And to all her sons and daughters
May they be strong and forever free
Let us live to protect her beauty
And look with pride on the golden dome
They say home is where the heart is
These green mountains are my home
These green mountains are my home

FAMOUS PEOPLE

Arthur, Chester A. (1829–1886), 21st U.S. president

Bradwell, Myra Colby (1831–1894), first U.S. female attorney

Coolidge, Calvin (1872–1933), 30th U.S. president

Davenport, Thomas (1802–1851), inventor

Deere, John (1804–1886), industrialist

Dewey, George (1837–1917), naval officer

Dewey, John (1859–1952), philosopher, psychologist, and educator

Douglas, Stephen A. (1813–1861), politician

Gibbons, Gail (1944–), children's author and illustrator

Hesse, Karen (1952–), children's author

Hunt, Richard Morris (1827–1895), architect

Hunt, William Morris (1824–1879), artist

Muldowney, Shirley (1940–), race car driver

Otis, Elisha Graves (1811–1861), inventor

Rockwell, Norman (1894–1978), painter and illustrator

Sanders, Bernie (1941–), senator

Sheehan, Patty (1956–), golfer

Smith, Joseph (1805–1844), religious leader

Stevens, Thaddeus (1792–1868), lawyer, politician, and abolitionist

Teter, Hannah (1987–), snowboarder

Wells, Henry (1805–1878), founded the American Express Company

WORDS TO KNOW

armory (AR-mur-ee) a place for making or storing guns and other weapons

colonists (KOL-uh-nists) people who settle a new land for their home country

immigrants (IM-uh-gruhnts) people who move from their home country into another country

industry (IN-duh-stree) a type of business

precision (pri-SI-zuhn) using exact measurements

quarry (KWOR-ee) an open area where building stone is cut out

republic (ri-PUB-lik) a form of government in which the people have the power to elect public officials

rural (RUR-uhl) in the countryside, outside of cities and towns

sap (SAP) a liquid that runs through plants

veterans (VET-ur-uhns) people who have participated in wars

TO LEARN MORE

IN THE LIBRARY

Dornfield, Margaret, William McGeveran, and Steven Otfinoski. *Vermont: The Green Mountain State*. New York, NY: Cavendish Square, 2016.

Krasner, Barbara. *Native Nations of the Northeast*. Mankato, MN: The Child's World, 2016.

LaPlante, Walter. *The Appalachian Trail*. New York, NY: Gareth Stevens, 2017.

ON THE WEB

Visit our Web site for links about Vermont:
childsworld.com/links

Note to Parents, Teachers, and Librarians: We routinely verify our Web links to make sure they are safe and active sites. So encourage your readers to check them out!

PLACES TO VISIT OR CONTACT
Vermont Vacation
vermontvacation.com
1 National Life Drive, 6th Floor
Montpelier, VT 05620
800/837-6668
For more information about traveling in Vermont

Vermont History Museum
vermonthistory.org/visit/vermont-history-museum
109 State Street
Montpelier, VT 05609
802/828-2291
For more information about the history of Vermont

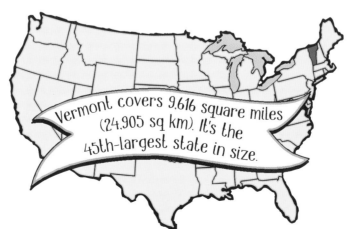

Vermont covers 9,616 square miles (24,905 sq km). It's the 45th-largest state in size.

INDEX

Bye, Green Mountain State. We had a great time. We'll come back soon!